Speak
YOUR
WAY
TO Purpose

A COLLECTION OF THOUGHTS
AND INSPIRATIONAL LIFE LESSONS
TO MOVE FORWARD

NICOLE O. SALMON

Printed in Canada

First Printing, 2015

ISBN: 978-0-9938420-8-5

Published by:

Conclusio House Publishing

10-8550 Torbram Rd.

Suite 430

Brampton, ON

L6T 0H7

www.conclusiohouse.com

This book is dedicated to my son, Makih L. Salmon. You are my number one fan and loudest cheerleader. If I preach a thousand sermons and write one hundred books, if I sit in seats of honour and speak before great men, you will still be the part of my life I am most proud of. You are an outstanding soul, a young man after God's own heart, and a pivotal part of my life's purpose.

Introduction

Discovering your purpose is one thing, staying in your purpose is a whole other ball game. I've lived my own exhausting cycle of getting fired up about my life's direction only to burst out the gate and be side-tracked by personal guilt from past mistakes, the discouraging look on the faces of those who can't figure out why I even desire to do the things I've set out to do, the fear of failure and humiliation, the fear of the responsibility of succeeding ... need I go on?

In each of those moments, I would hear God's voice reaffirming my passion as it relates to what I was called and gifted to do , but each time, like clockwork, I'd get a few steps on track and then lose momentum all over again.

As a facilitator and life coach (and especially as a mother), I am always urging people to write things down. So why wasn't I capturing those powerful conversations between my soul and Heaven? Why wasn't I documenting the lessons that made sense of my darkest moments and the words of life that rescued me from my most despairing encounters with life? There was no reason. So I did just that. I began to write and record these moments and thoughts. Sometimes on the noisy bus ride to work, sometimes in the middle of a fiery Sunday morning service, and sometimes between bites while having dinner with friends. Whenever a moment of insight struck, I wrote it down.

But the power wasn't in writing down what I was learning. The true power was released when I began to speak[3(1)] it back to myself. I realized that for a long time I was living, but not learning. I was acquiring a well of knowledge, but not drawing and drinking from it. Speaking my way to purpose meant that I would now drink form that well. I started to revisit the well on dry days, hard days, throw-in-the-towel days, hide-under-a-rock days; and in speaking to myself, I was learning and drawing strength. I was maintaining momentum. I was staying in purpose.

The distraction to give in never goes away. But we can take those prophetic words and use them like a bungee cord to snap back whenever we feel like we're going over the edge. As we live life from a place of purpose, there needs to be a reduction in our bounce-back time.

Remember the last few times you disobeyed God and stepped out of purpose? You probably cried yourself a river, and pity-partied yourself into the wee hours of the night. Maybe you got so mad at yourself that you placed a muzzle on your soul. You cannot waste another year, week, or day on the sidelines regretting where you went wrong. You must learn and leave. It's a diversion strategy that the purpose-predator, Satan, uses to suppress what the purpose-planter,

---

1 speak[3] [amplified verb] 1) a divine utterance of words that is heard in both the earth and in heavenly places, 2) possessing the ability to impact the present and the future, 3) having physical, emotional, and spiritual properties, 4) carrying a message originating from the Triune God of heaven and earth.

God, has placed inside of you. Your mistake is over. God has long cleared the path for you, so it is time to get back in alignment with your God-design.

This book is an invitation to tear down the caution tape, get back into purpose, and stay there.

How to Use This Book

The following pages won't read like a how-to book; rather, it is a collection of Spirit-inspired thoughts, life lessons, words of encouragement, and declarations that God has used to anchor me in purpose. When you read something that resonates with you, change it into the first person and speak[3] it out loud. Sounds silly? Well, so is the negative self-talk you've probably had with yourself for the past few years about why purpose has skipped over you and why it is not yours for the taking. Our words are seeds, and what we sow in speaking will manifest in reaping.

Welcome to my Well,

Here are 7 ways to maximize your reading experience:

1. Friends and Family – Read with a friend or group of friends. *Speak Your Way to Purpose* makes a great conversation starter or book club read.

2. Daily Devotions – Read a thought daily as a part of your regular devotions.

3. Team Building – Start your next meeting by sharing an entry with your team. Lead a discussion on what your organization or ministry will do that week to stay aligned with the team's collective purpose.

4. Fasting and Prayer – Dedicate a set time to fast about your own struggles with staying in purpose. Choose a thought per day to focus on as you spend time in prayer.

5. Meditation – Read a thought followed by a quiet time of listening and reflecting in God's presence.

6. Journaling – Read and journal your heart's response in your *Write Your Way to Purpose* Journal.

7. Social Media – Post, Tweet, or Vlog about the entry that has impacted you the most with the hashtag #speak3

Purpose–you won't get it, until you get it. Much of life seems aimless and unsatisfying when we do not make a solid connection with purpose, the reason for which we were created. Purpose is not something that we find, like a displaced object that is external to us, but rather something we live out from an authentic place that already exists on the inside of us.

When the creation, the Creator, and the calling reunite, a kinetic connection occurs, which begins an inward and upward realignment. We will no longer sit still and do life the same way we used to. Our entire being and all our efforts will shift from wandering aimlessly to being strategic arrows shot in a specific direction for an intended end.

It's a new season! Even if you feel like your old self, the expectation of God's Word is not that you *feel*, but that you *follow*.

Look for the *lesson.* Even your most despairing moments hold valuable insight for your next level.

Fear can be crippling, but not nearly as haunting as regret. *Trust* your instinct, but more importantly, trust your God.

As you live authentically, according to your God-design, it will ignite some to pursue the path of purpose, and invite others to criticize. Both are indications that you are *progressing* well.

Purpose is about the *life* you live, the life you give, and the life you leave.

Who envisioned a season and a process as challenging as what you have gone through? God knew exactly what this journey would entail, yet He still whispered "*Come.*" You did not hear wrong. You are exactly where you need to be.

Sometimes you have to keep your peace to keep the *peace.*

Support is not eternal; it is seasonal. Don't be upset when people come and go. God knows exactly what and who you need to cultivate your calling.

Never let your fear of the unknown keep you from the *adventure* of your life.

They say, "Great minds think alike." Actually, great minds think differently. But together, purpose is propelled into *motion.*

It will be an ongoing challenge to turn down opportunities that your gifts would seemingly be an asset to. Remember, some openings are windows for insight, not doors for passage.

The *success* of the purpose-inspired journey is dependent on:

1. Your ability to discern between what is good for you and what is best for you
2. Your ability to conserve your energy for that which is purpose-pleasing (God-focused), rather than people-pleasing (man-focused)
3. Your courage to avoid guilt traps—the places people will try to guilt you into because you are "capable."

Focus is good, but avoid tunnel vision. If you look up, there is much to be celebrated.

Low *expectations* rob us of what God intended us to have. You may be on the right journey to the right destination, but why take an economy-class trip when God has already purchased first-class seating?

"They" and "everyone" don't really exist. The seeming majority is often the *minority.*

Do not be moved by the wind of man's persuasive words; instead, be carried in the direction of your *purpose* by the current of the Holy Spirit.

Dig deeper. It's there, but you won't uncover it by standing still.

Trying to find your purpose? What has God *graced* you to do that only you can do? What's that sweet spot that terrifies other people, but is simple to you because of His grace?

God is not looking for perfection. He is drawn to the *sincere* heart that desires to be perfected.

Doing what's popular will bring you fans. Doing what's *right* will bring you favour.

The discipline of *solitude* makes room for your spirit to hear and be heard. There's so much that God wants to reveal to you, but you must make the time to *be still* and listen.

Sometimes you'll have to ask God, "Why am I doing this, again?" And when you do, He'll allow your shallow reserve to become a *roaring resolve.*

Ever heard the saying, "Keep digging until you hit gold"? Well I say, "Keep digging until you hit oil." Throughout Scripture, oil is symbolic of the Holy Spirit. Its application denotes consecration, covering, blessing, ordination, and Holy Spirit power. The task before you requires much more than pragmatism, natural abilities, giftedness, and strategic planning. You need the *Oil.*

Don't desire what's easy; instead, desire what is *lasting.*

Have you been holding out on God because stepping out in the direction of purpose did not land you the outcome you expected? There is always a *lesson.* What might God be trying to teach you through your disappointment?

Declare:

I may not always get it right, but
I'm *committed* to the process.

It may seem like you've been waiting forever. But be assured that it will come to you at the *right time.* What's yours will not miss you.

Don't accept average; it's not in your DNA. Your internal GPS will always direct you towards *greatness.*

Fight the urge to fear adventure or resist change. Fear keeps close company with remorse, and cohabitates with regret.

When we allow our experiences to be unpacked, fine-tuned, and made clearer, and when we move out from under the rubble of fear, failure, and the misappropriation of purpose, our *true journey* will begin.

You can do it. Your frustration is an indication that you are *close.*

People-watching will lead to insanity. Set your gaze on the *One* who called you.

Those who are seemingly more successful than you do not necessarily possess more substance on the inside than you do. They have just mastered the *discipline* of putting what they have to work.

Pursue who you've been *called* to be,
without apology or compromise.

Carrying a complex load of duty and responsibility requires that you take time out to have a good laugh and a good cry. Each represents your growing ability to be vulnerable. Allow yourself to *feel*. When you cry, it's usually because you feel weak, defeated, or broken, and that is okay. Each tear provides those emotions with a detoxifying escape from your soul. *Laughter* helps you to relax and take life a little less seriously. Shame is debilitating, but your ability to laugh in those moments when things don't turn out right is powerful beyond measure.

Finding your way to purpose will require *circumventing* the path that the well-intentioned have carved out for you.

It’s risky, but it’s ***worth*** it.

Sometimes they will celebrate you, and sometimes you will go without praise. But each time your calling remains *true.*

Sometimes you will feel like a success, and sometimes you will feel like you've made a huge mistake. But each time your calling remains *true.*

Do not succumb to the paralysis of *perfectionism.* Throw yourself in, uncertainties and all.

We were created in the ***image of God.*** And because you bear His image, there is no more need to question if what is inside of you is valuable, worth pursuing, or worth sharing.

No more 'one foot in the water and one foot on land.' It's time to go *all in.*

There is no need to *strive* for the sake of proving something to the world. Our Father has assured us that we have nothing to prove. Instead, our greatest accomplishment is in harnessing what He has given us and using it to serve.

You will often feel overlooked. Recognize it as *divine covering.* God may be providing a shield or some much needed shade.

As you begin to build, there will be many distractions. But as a good workman, never put your tools down, and never put your project on hold. Continue to *work* with what God has placed in your hands.

Whenever we leave from underneath the covering where God has placed us, we become an open target for the enemy. Therefore, stay in your *lane* until He gives you the signal to cross.

God is saving you from yourself. The calling on your life is God's investment, and He protects what is His. It is both human and a spiritual warfare tactic to feel as though your faults, failures, and imperfections will shut you out of what God has for you. You don't have to be a tragic hero, undone by characteristics that serve as your strength but also your weakness at times. The best of you will be the *test* of you as He refines you for greatness.

Don't allow your energies to be diverted. There are many things you *can* do, but it is important to first focus on the things that you *should* do.

Do you realize the significance of what you were called to do? Once it is *released* it can still be heard long after you have stopped speaking, and can be felt long after your hands have ceased their labour.

In case it seems like God has had a memory lapse concerning the gifts, dreams, and promises He's made concerning you, remember He says, "I will not forget you." The Hebrew verb used suggests an even stronger assurance—"I am *unable* to forget you!"

Most people think that purpose happens when you find yourself. In truth, purpose is actualized, for the believer, when we *lose* ourselves and give what little is left away.

Prayer, simply put, is a *conversation* between us and God. We speak, He answers. He speaks, we obey.

Declare:

I will ***produce*** out of the abundance of my gifting this year!

An *attitude* shift will give you an aptitude lift.

If the King of kings could be born in a smelly stable, surely you don't need to be *perfect* for the King to use your life to reveal His glory.

Sometimes a "No" in the earth is a resounding *"Yes!"* in the heavens.

You would never leave a newborn baby unattended; likewise, don't walk away from your *vision* until it is fully grown.

Today's *storm* is forming tomorrow's biceps.

Endeavour to *learn* the lesson the first time around. We are deceived in thinking we have all the time in the world. We arrogantly put off for next year what we were not diligent in pursuing this year.

There is a strategic grooming that takes place when we are hard pressed by life's uncomfortable encounters. When we fail to learn and, more importantly, live out the intended lesson, we come full circle and face them again. *Time* is promised to no one. Therefore, learn the lesson the first time around so that you can maximize your time on Earth.

Don't be discouraged; your mistakes haven't disqualified you from God's plan. They have simply *qualified* you for His grace and mercy.

The Spirit is speaking. Carve out some time to *hear* what He has to say.

Trust God's plan for your life. Outside of it your spirit can't breathe, and nothing you do will prosper.

What? Give up? Don't allow someone else to cause you to walk away so easily. You have more *gumption* in you than that.

You'll know you're in alignment with your God-design when you're exhausted, put your hands to the task and you'll find yourself coming to *life.*

It is so easy to become consumed with the 'could've, should've, would've.' But every time we open our eyes, it is another invitation to *walk* in purpose.

The magic is in the things you got wrong, not in the things you got right. Notice the scrutiny you place yourself under when you don't achieve the success you intended on? It is under this microscope that you become a student of *success.*

The proud man says, "Look what I can do." The wise man says, "Look what God has gifted me to do." Your *shining* is not arrogance; it is your purpose coming forth.

It is your imperfections that make you a powerful force to reckon with. Your vulnerabilities open you up to God in a way that your standing tall and confident cannot. You become the little child He desires you to be, desperately seeking guidance, covering, and support. It is from this uncertain, unknowing place that your reliance on the unseen God stirs the supernatural of *Jehovah Shammah*, the Lord is Present.

Are you feeling under intense pressure today? Then maybe it is the time appointed for you to *push* and give birth to what's on the inside.

No matter how much you suppress them, purpose and calling cannot be turned off. At the right moment, life will place a demand on your *gifting.*

Today is a *you-can-make-it* kind of day.

Losing a battle is not the same as losing the war. Don't be discouraged. *Continue* on the path of purpose.

When God says "Yes," and life answers with a "No," *Knock Again.*

When you cease to appreciate, you begin to depreciate. Value is not determined by what you have, but rather it is measured by your ability to *appreciate* what you have been given.

Seek every opportunity to find *value* in your valley; you may discover that you are actually standing on your mountain peak.

Don't slacken your pace because the pressure has lessened. Use those quiet seasons that feel like purpose is on pause to your advantage. They've been carved out for you as *respites* to refuel and refocus.

Someone was hoping that last storm would crush you. They didn't know you were *built* to last.

If you've tasted purpose, then you know that the next best thing to living out yours is to gain *momentum* by walking alongside someone who is living out theirs.

Purpose is not a single destination; rather, it is a series of purposeful pit stops you make as you journey through life with *intention.*

Declare:

I will no longer walk around tormented by my past, frustrated with my present, and doubting my *future.*

Purpose—your flesh and your logic may not recognize it, but your spirit does. What do you do that causes the most timid part of you to *leap* about wildly?

Show *kindness* when the most rational response is revenge. In doing so, you generate a good harvest for your next level.

When you put yourself out there and your efforts are not received, don't shrink, *strive*—make strenuous efforts towards your goal.

Although we know that God has the power to fulfill the dreams and aspirations that He himself has planted in us, there are times when the colliding of faith and failure leads to us questioning the All-Powerful Yahweh. *Faith* in God is the bridge between the despair we perceive with our senses and the seemingly nonsensical next steps we discern in the Spirit.

We almost always know what's needed in a difficult situation. What we lack is not insight, but the *courage* to do what is right.

You won't be transformed overnight; but every day, one obedient response at a time, you're *changing.*

Maturity is the ability to hear people tearing your reputation to pieces, and not let it throw you off your game. Turn criticism, both negative and constructive, into *fuel.*

Don't focus on being a star; focus more on being a *light.*

We spend so much time trying to avoid the hard places, but destiny and purpose are *refined* in life's hard places

Can you feel when your spiritual meter is low? When you've become short-tempered with family and friends, and life starts to feel unbearable, heavy, and confusing. Life is demanding, and there is always so much to do that, if we are not careful, time with God can become just another item on our never-ending to-do list.

Alone time with God is integral to cultivating purpose. Yet, though we know this spiritual truth, there we stand, unmoved, not taking the time we so desperately need. The strength and direction we need cannot be found in chaos. *Prayer* is pivotal, but *listening* is essential.

When God puts a stop to your plans, it's not called failure, it's called ***intervention.***

What's inside of you was intended to be a driving *force.* Standing still is a waste of compounding energy, and a fire hazard in the making. There is too much fire in your locomotive to stand still.

If you say you can't, you won't. If you say He can, *He will.*

There's a difference between dead and delayed. Pray that God reveals to you what is dead in your life and what is yet on its *way.*

Until God *shifts* you from where you are, put what's in your hand to work.

The soul has a natural longing for times of retreat. There is a constant pulling and tugging on the inside to come away. But life, like a pit of quicksand, can suck purpose in. We can become so busy with purpose that it drowns out the Spirit's voice as He bids us to come and sit at His feet. It is in moments of *spirit-filled solitude* that purpose is kindled.

Don't be deceived or distracted; *momentary* gain is often followed by consequential pain.

The difference between vain repetition and focused *consistency* is vision and purpose.

The pressure won't kill you. It's simply turning your hard places into *diamonds.*

The *change* we desire will occur when we want it more than we want our comfort zone.

You don't have to be perfect to pursue your purpose. *Pursuing* your purpose will bring about the perfecting process.

Release is imperative. The great and tragic wonder of the Dead Sea is that it has a continuous stream of fresh water flowing into it, but nothing ever flows out. This one-way flow results in the Dead Sea being oversaturated with salt. In the same way, the life that bottles up purpose becomes a wading pool of toxicity.

When you can see but have no *vision*,
the loss of insight is the true disability.

Give a name to your *calling* and own it. Add personality and character to it. Furnish it and invest in it. You serve purpose no justice by making apologies for it and acting as though it doesn't exist.

Losing doesn't always mean you've lost. Sometimes it is the *best* thing that could happen to you.

Declare:

Each day, and with every opportunity that presents itself, I will make *choices* that reflect who I will become tomorrow

This, right here, is about more than creating the kind of life you want to live. It's about carving out a path and leaving a *legacy* that will inspire generations

Don't be concerned that your life doesn't follow a linear, methodical path. Life happens in a beautiful *rhythm* of ups and downs.

This season will require more energy than you have to give, a greater load than you have muscles to carry, and more resources than you have in your bank account. But don't let this scare you or send you running back to your comfort zone. God is increasing your capacity for *greatness*, expanding your faith to leap mountains, and positioning you for an increase you cannot contain.

Resist the temptation to feed your need for speed. *Steady* consistency wins the race.

Insight brings you an awareness of the darkness around you. Introspection challenges you to confront the darkness *within* you.

No longer be motived by how you *feel.* Emotions are cardinal liars. They are informed by your past, intimidated by your present, and petrified at the thought of your future.

Life will ask of you, time and time again, "Are you sure you are really called?" If permitted to speak, your moments of imperfection would testify against you, "She/he doesn't have what it takes." But don't allow a moment of weakness to dictate your *response.*

The moment you stop living for the validation of others is the moment you start to truly *live.*

As a Spirit-led soul, you will be drawn into seasons of being still. Do not misread the slowing of your pace as purpose coming to a stop. God has not left you. God has not gone silent. God is at work, and you are growing during this season. Strength is gained when you work, but growth takes place when you *rest.*

The *breakthrough* you're looking for might seem out of reach, but if you stop now, you'll miss it.

You must be convicted of your calling. *Conviction* carries a stronger commitment than just being persuaded. It also speaks of being in agreement with your calling, which means that on the days when you don't feel it, see it, or even bear the slightest resemblance to it, your answer will remain "Yes!"

God will often call you to do the opposite of what seems logical or necessary. Have *faith* and follow.

In spite of that utterly lost feeling you may be experiencing right now, God knows your exact location and your exact *destination.*

Socrates said, "Beware the barrenness of a busy life." Activity and *productivity* are not the same thing. A clear sense of purpose will help you to differentiate between the two.

We all want someone we can follow—a mentor, a guide, a guru, a sage of some sort. Someone who has made the pilgrimage and back from where we desire to be, and has conquered our worst nightmares, with the battle scars to prove it. So, *follow Jesus.* It's what He asked of those rugged, unlearned fishermen before He transformed them into the leaders of the early church, Kingdom beneficiaries, and spiritual giants. And it's what He's asking of you today.

Your life may look nothing like what you expected. But every twist and turn, high and low, has made for a more *scenic* ride.

Continue to dream big, and continue to share those dreams with big thinkers. Those who are satisfied and content with the ho-hum of the ordinary life will never be able to identify with your quest for the *extraordinary.*

It could always be worse. Take time to recognize and give thanks for God's goodness and mercy in your life. That *last breath* you just took could have been the last breath you took. However, you are alive for a purpose. Now go find it and live it with unapologetic exuberance.

Don’t let the guilt of your past cause you to think small. Grab a hold of your destiny and dream again.

Don't mistake your good for great, when God has *spectacular* waiting for you just on the other side of your current situation.

Abraham's journey sent him in pursuit of a land he did not know. One would have described his orientation as being lost. Later on, we learn that his journey was not only in the direction of purpose, but also the precursor to his legacy.

Purpose is that *divine moment* when you leave the safety of home—your mental and/or physical safe place—and trust the navigation of the unseen God to an unfamiliar place.

Work while you *grow.* Waiting to mature before you pursue your purpose will only abort the seed.Even though life has given you a thousand blows, you are still victorious.

When moving in the direction of your purpose, exhaustion will suggest that you relapse into a familiar and destructive pattern. But don't subject yourself to another lap around the track when you're already so close to the *finish line.*

There is a unique relationship between pain and purpose. There will be pain in your purpose, and there will be purpose in your *pain.*

Don't fake who you are to meet the expectations of others. Be *authentic*, it's a refreshing drink for the thirsty soul.

Declare:

I bear the Spirit of the Creator. It is in my DNA to *produce.* I may flounder, but I will not fail.

Some of us have had to fight for so long that we've overlooked the power and the peace that can only be found in *surrender.*

God says, "If only you could *see* the view from up here."

Sometimes you slip, and sometimes you may detour willingly, but each time He forgives you and calls you His *own.*

You can fight back, or you can turn your back on the fight. They are both viable options. You must discern between *worth it* and worthless.

What's holding you back? If parting with it won't cost you a night's sleep, then *let it go.*

When your absolute best doesn't feel good enough, that's when the *magic* happens. The Spirit of God is released and increased in those moments of deficit.

Pay attention to the storm; it is an indication that you have just set your foot down in the right *direction.*

You must become a master engineer at tuning out distractions in order for the unsung melody of your life to be *heard.*

Sometimes you get exactly what you want, only to find out it is not what you *need.*

Your best thinking happens outside of the *crowd.*

Never choose comfort over *calling.*

You could choose what's easy, fall back on what's comfortable, or lean on what's familiar; but there is no *honour* in that.

When you stray away, don't stay away. God is waiting for your *return.* He is waiting for you to begin again and to pick up the vision from where you left off.

The journey you are on won't make sense to most people. At times it won't even make sense to you. But take courage, and practise the power of *speaking your way to purpose.*

Final Thoughts

Now it's time to fill your own well. I'm sure that as you read each page you could sense God's presence ministering to where you are specifically. You probably connected with your own moments of learning, when God's Spirit confirmed what He was already speaking to you before you picked up this book. The invitation is extended—write them down in your *Write Your Way to Purpose* notebook. Remember, the power isn't just in writing down what you are learning; the true power is released when you begin to **speak**[3].

About the Author

Nicole O. Salmon is a Personal Development & Life Coach who specializes in maximizing individual and corporate success through the art of cultivating potential and growing synergistic teams. As a minister, Nicole's reflective coaching technique, coupled with her one-to-one and group facilitation sessions, has led scores of professionals and organizations alike to a place of lasting success and high-level efficiency. She is the proud mother of one son, Makih L. Salmon, an intelligent and talented young man in whom she delights. Together, they live a full and exciting life in Toronto, Ontario.